ONE MAN'S WAR

1916 - 1918

by
Horace Smethurst

One Man's War. 1916 - 1918

© AURORA PUBLISHING

ISBN: 1 85926 052 7

Distributed by: Aurora Enterprises Ltd.
Unit 9, Bradley Fold Trading Estate,
Radcliffe Moor Road,
Bradley Fold,
BOLTON BL2 6RT
Tel: 01204 370753/2
Fax: 01204 370751

Thanks to: Ian Smethurst, Bolton, for offering
Horace Smethurst's notebook for publication.

Edited by: Dawn G Robinson-Walsh.

*Printed
and bound by*:   Manchester Free Press,
Unit E3, Longford Trading Estate,
Thomas Street,
Stretford,
Manchester M32 0JT.

ONE MAN'S WAR

We are privileged to have access to the notebook of Horace Smethurst, born on 10th April, 1894, who joined the army and fought on the Western Front in France and Belgium during the Great War of 1914-18.

There are many books available telling the detailed history of and lead up to World War I, but it surely increases our understanding to be able to read the personal accounts and real life experiences of those involved in the event which for many of us is beyond full comprehension.

Anyone who has read the work of the War Poets will have some idea of how grim trench warfare was; likewise, those who have visited places like Ypres where Horace spent some of his time at the Front before sustaining a head injury which was to send him home, will have some idea of the grim nature of the ordeal of the War. The notebook contains limited information, because it was compiled largely from letters home, with details pieced together, and as in all wars, correspondence was always subject to censorship, "the blue pencil". Therefore, we miss out on much of the military detail and descriptions of the true horrors of the war from which many young men never returned. Even so, we can go some way towards imagining the noise, the sleepless exhaustion, the infestation by lice and the generally appalling conditions during the short but intensive stints in the Front Line.

What prevails throughout Horace's account is an optimism which perhaps kept him going, an attempt to see the positive side of events, to make the most of what was available, and an unfailing sense of duty and belief in what had to be done. Rarely throughout his notebook does he complain, although perhaps this is because it was mainly written for his family. Through the book, we see the various aspects of war: the training at home and abroad, the sports and activities held to build men's morale, and the action in the midst of shell-fire and gas attack.

Horace was one of the lucky ones. He did his duty and returned home to marry his wife Mary Elizabeth (known as Polly) and to father three children, Thomas, Herbert and Joyce, although we do not know what the long term effects of his experience and injury may have been. To many soldiers, Horace was extremely fortunate to receive an injury bad enough to send him back to "blighty", but not to kill him - deliverance from the hell of trench warfare.

To many, the First World War was one of the most horrible wars in European history, partly because it seemed to be mainly the result of pointless power struggles between rulers of nation states. As always, the men who had to fight the War were not the ones who made the decision to do so. The rat-infested trenches stretched across western Europe, and the ground between the trenches became like deserts of mud with no life, and the dying throes of wounded men, many of whom suffocated. The War was mainly a defensive one with progress hindered by machine-gun fire, barbed wire, and poisonous gas, which made it a long, drawn out series of battles.

Despite the futility of this particular War, social attitudes were such that young men went willingly, or were condemned as cowards if they did not take up the uniform. The War had great cost-not only economically-but in the three million men who perished and the further three million who were left permanently maimed. Perhaps the worst of it was that these heavy casualties and losses were apparently destroyed for no real purpose.

Dawn Robinson-Walsh

Horace Smethurst

Contents

"Sombre the night is.
And though we have our lives, we know
What sinister threat lurks there"

Extract taken from
"Returning, We Hear the Larks" - Isaac Rosenberg,
1917 who was killed in action on the Western Front
on 1st April, 1918.

HORACE'S NOTEBOOK
1916-1918

12th. December, 1916 - *Windsor*

At last! The hour has struck when I must push aside all personal considerations, curb my ambitions, cease my studies, and obey the mandate of my country. With millions of my country-men, I must become a soldier and take up arms to maintain our country's prestige and uphold her honour; to protect the rights and liberties we enjoy for which our fore-fathers fought and bled; to guard the shores of our native land; and stem the onrush of the mighty hordes of enemies, the most formidable foe the world has ever seen, of a ruthless and unscrupulous despot and his minions who desire to dominate the whole of Europe, aye, even the whole world; if they could virtually enslave its people, dictate its policy and mould its destiny.

Therefore, on 1st December, 1916, I proceed to Bolton, then on to Preston, where at the public hall I am classed as A1, am despatched to Fulwood Barracks and am duly posted to the Household Battalion, 2nd Life Guards, stationed at Combermere Barracks, Windsor and then return home for the night. On the morning of 5th December, I report at Fulwood Barracks, receive my passport, entrain at Preston, and am whistled through space at express speed up to the great metropolis, the capital of England. I then entrain for Windsor, where I arrive late at night after a long and rather exciting journey. I am admitted, and along with scores of others in "civvies" have my first experience of a soldier's life by sleeping on the floor of the Barracks but with plenty of blankets to make me fairly comfortable. My brain seems in a whirl and everything is strange, for it is the beginning of a new life and as I lay wrapped in my blankets in the stillness of the night, thoughts come and go like flashes of lightning, and I wonder what the future has in store for me when the morning dawns. At length, I compose myself and drowsiness seizes my senses and I fall away into slumber land.

At early morn, I am roused from my slumbers by the shrill note of the bugle sounding the Reveille, and springing from the folds of my blankets I feel refreshed after my first sleep in a Barracks. At 6.30am, I sit down with a keen appetite and enjoy a good breakfast of porridge, ham and bread, and tea. For several days, I am confined to Barracks with nothing to do but look round, but that is no hardship, for there is plenty to see and to occupy one's mind.

On the journey, I passed Windsor Castle, but it was dark, and I could only form a faint idea as to its surroundings, but from what I can see of Windsor in the day-time from the Barrack windows, it appears to be a nice place.

On 9th December, I passed the Doctor and became Trooper 2214 of the Regiment. Things up to now have seemed rather mixed but I am doing nicely and feel in the pink. The food is good and the accommodation excellent. My nervousness is gradually wearing off, and I feel more settled. All our instructors come from the Guards Brigade, the pay is good, and one is expected to keep up a good and smart appearance. As yet, I have had no parades, but I have got my khaki suit, and expect to go out this afternoon for my first look round.

21st. December, 1916 - *Windsor*

My short experience of Barracks life shows me that it is not all beer and skittles, nor roses and sweetmeats, although there is plenty of fun and jollity as well as hard work and one soon learns to take things as they come along. Here, one comes into contact with all sorts and conditions of men, of varied temperaments and dispositions, and from all parts of the country. There are optimists, pessimists, humourists and philosophers, all assembled together and each looks at the business from his own point of view; but all are here for one purpose-that of being moulded into soldiers so as to be able sooner or later each to take his part in the game of war.

Here, everything is kept spotlessly clean, for the final business of a soldier is to make himself spruce and smart. It is clean, clean, clean all day long which makes one feel fit. It hardens the muscles and is, I suppose, the initial or preliminary opening to something more arduous in the nature of preparation for the great ordeal. This morning, the sun is shining beautifully and there is promise of a lovely day. It is the day for general swabbing-cleaning and putting straight our beds, and equipment, cleaning floors, tables, windows, doors, polishing brasses; in fact, making everything clean and in order. I am writing these lines in our room which is very nice and tidy, for the officer may at any moment pop in for room inspection.

To a recruit, the Drill Sergeant appears a most formidable person, and the embodiment of evil, for he strikes terror into some of their hearts. He is considered to be the back-bone of the Army, for without his aid it would simply be in a state of chaos. To him is entrusted largely the work of making the raw material into a machine that will do the work required. A conglomeration of all sorts and shapes are placed in his hands, some straight, some crooked, others with more chest at the back than front, but all must be made as one, so that when inspection time comes, the Sergeant may get the reward he seeks in the laconic ejaculations such as "Good, Very Smart, You May Dismiss Them!"

I may here observe that Squad Drill means learning to salute and dress properly; to form into line on the right or left, on the march, or at the double. We may here imagine that a Squad is on the Barrack Square and the Instructor, by his manner and scrutinizing gaze as he eyes the men over seems to convey the following remarks: now then, look at me. I am your Father. If you follow my advice, and do as I tell you, smartly, I will make you into men. If you don't, then the devil will take you as his own. Then, after a few explanations as to how things should be done, he commences his work. Each man tries to be as smart as possible, but through nervousness oversteps the mark, and makes a bloomer. The Sergeant's eye is over on the roll, and as he spies one looking upwards instead of to the front, bawls out: "What are you looking up there for man? You'll never go to heaven. Look to your front. Right, left, left, left". Sometimes when on the march he will spy someone looking on the floor and will roar out: "You there. What are you looking down there for? You've lost no money, you spent it at the canteen last night. Look to your front". And with such humorous remarks as these, we are gradually initiated into the evolutions of the drill.

Christmas is near, and we are wondering who will be the lucky ones to get leave. However, only a few are being granted, so the rest of us will have to spend Christmas in Barracks, and try to have a good time. We are now on Foot and Swedish Drill, which is no doubt intended to loosen the limbs, make us supple, and give us a springy step. I have also a rifle and rumour says that we shall shortly be on rifle drill. I am feeling in the pink, getting nicely into the run of things and intend, whatever comes my way, to put my heart into it, do my best and try to come out on top.

Sunday, I had a walk through a pretty little village just outside Windsor. There is a very nice church and a beautifully set out graveyard, which in summertime must be a paradise, for it is pleasing to the eye even now at this time of the year.

I received on the 28th a parcel, letter and card posted on 22nd which evidently has been delayed. I came across a young man named Hallam from my village who is in the Coldstream Guards and was very pleased to see someone from home. Christmas is over once more, and I had a good one in the Barracks. We had a fine feed of potatoes, meat and vegetables, Christmas pudding, bread and cheese, oranges and were given cigarettes. In the evening, we had a grand concert with our band taking part in the programme and I assure you that it was really a splendid Christmas time. I am not exactly feeling A1 on account of having again been inoculated, but it has not affected me once. I have been vaccinated once and inoculated twice and have two days off parades in consequence. I am seated before a nice, warm fire and console myself with the thought that I have now finished with that part of the business.

I have had a route march, a splendid walk of about seven miles in the Great Park which is a perfectly straight road, beginning at the Windsor Castle Gates and at the other end of which is a copper-horse, a fine statue of George IV on horse-back. This park is about 20 miles in circumference and is very much like a forest, where thousands of deer roam about at their leisure.

It is now 18th January, and for about a month we have

had very bad weather. Rain, snow, frost and wind; in fact, everything that is capable of making one feel uncomfortable; still, I am in good form, and one has to put up with these things, for there is no way out of the difficulty. I have again had a mid-night removal, and this time not to the hook, but to No. 1 Osborne Villas, and have also been transferred back to the No. 2 Company. It is a common sight to see and very amusing to watch men moving from one place to another. Nearly 500 men have been added to our battalion since I joined, and men must daily be moved to make room for the new-comers. There are between twelve and thirteen hundred men in our battalion, and I understand that more are to be added later. After all, life has its features and phases of interest and humour, as well as of hard and almost continuous work.

11th. February, 1917 - *Windsor*

The initial or preliminary course of my instruction in Squad Drill is now completed, and I am up against the most important and essential part of my training: the use of arms. This will involve some hard and strenuous work, but I am prepared to face the music, weather the storm and expect to emerge from the ordeal with credit.

For several days our company has spent most of the time in Windsor Park, in the snow at company drill. The inclement weather which has prevailed of late, is now slightly on the improve, for today the sun is shining brightly, making the snow glint like crystals. Company drill is much more complicated, and to me it is very interesting. A company is divided into platoons, and platoons into sections, and it is a sight to see each part working out its own formation. We will take the Artillery formation. This formation is used when a company comes under artillery fire, and its object is to reduce the possibility of casualties to a minimum. There are four platoons in this formation, no.1 straight ahead, no.2 to the right, no. 3 to the left and no. 4 about turn; so that they form thus.

Then, each platoon breaks off as the company has done, until the men are scattered over a wide area, and instead of being in bunches, are just units here and there. Such are the movements in artillery formation.

On Monday, I commenced my course of musketry, which is very interesting work (with the emphasis on the work) for it is the hardest work I have done since I joined the Army. Of course, it is new, and in consequence, until one gets the knack of handling the rifle, it is difficult. The rifle only weighs 8½lbs but there is no stretching the point in saying that, at times, it almost gets the strongest man down. It is the various attitudes one has to assume, and the different movements in the handling of the rifle that count. Sometimes, one relaxes one's efforts on account of feeling a little tired, and handles the rifle rather gingerly, but the roving eye of the instructor spots this and he at once roars out: "What is the matter man? Are you tired? Or are you afraid of breaking the rifle? You've no need to be. Bang it about. If you do break it we will give you another", and thus, the game goes on.

The strenuous routine of the work is somewhat relieved in observing the peculiar attitudes and mannerisms of the instructors when at drill. Each has a style and manner of his own in imparting and impressing his instructions on the men, and they are all in earnest, as they know that their reputations as smart instructors depends on the quality and smartness of the men under their tuition, so they vie with each other as to who can turn out the smartest Squad. At one point of the Square, you may see a fine, well-built, dark complexioned man, straight as an arrow, an eye that seems to pierce you through, and a long, heavy, drooping moustache. There he stands like a statue and in a loud voice like the roar of a lion, gives the command. The men spring up smartly and execute the movement as if electrified. At another point may be seen a stout, florid complexioned instructor, with a harsh rasping voice who gives his commands in a jerky, staccato manner, moving backwards and forwards with the Squad just as if the execution of the movement depended on the actions of his body, but the result is the same for it is executed with smartness and precision.

Our instructor is a smart, genial Irishman named McLaughlin, a "real borth of a bhoy" from the Coldstream Guards, who addresses us as follows: "now bhoys, I want you to be smart, to do as I tell you, and I will pull you through. Do ye mind bhoys, that all the men in my regiment are smart, in fact, we are considered to be the smartest in the Brigaded Guards, for they are always doing something. Even when in barracks, they are cleaning buttons, or brushing their clothes, all to make them look quite smart and spruce; and not standing about in groups arguin' the 'pint' about nothing. Now remember bhoys what I have told yez: when you get the word of command, put a bit of jerk into it and spring up smartly". Having "gingered" us up, he then with clenched hands, a slight stoop forward, and apparently half-closed eyes, 'though seeing us all the time, in a sharp incisive tone gives the command which is executed with smartness and alacrity.

Next week, we go on the miniature range in the barracks for actual firing practice. The following week, we proceed to Runnymede, where I shall do my best and hope to come out with a decent record. Runnymede is a small island in the River Thames, not far from Windsor.

It is now 19th February and the weather for several days has been very wet, making everything under foot muddy and dirty, but one has to make the best of prevailing circumstances and conditions, and I am glad to say that all is going well. This morning we went to Runnymede for ball firing practice. Service rifles and cartridges are used which is quite different from firing on the miniature range, with miniature rifles and shot. It is a rare sensation when one lets drive with the first service cartridge; and one has to grip the rifle firmly and press the butt end well into the shoulder in order to counteract the recoil or else get a nasty bruised shoulder by its impact. However, like everything else the nervousness gradually wears off and efficiency comes by practice. Each man fires 20 rounds, 10 at 100 yards, and 10 at 200 yards; my first five rounds were quite off the mark, but before I had finished, there was a decided improvement in my shooting. Thursday next is the day for "firing" Classification Tests and I hope to do well, for the scores on that day are the ones that count. The classifications are: up to 55 points-3rd class; up to 90 points-2nd class; up to 125 points-1st class and over 125 points-Marksman.

A draft is going out from here tomorrow, Tuesday, 20th. February. The leave I am expecting will be my draft leave, for I shall probably be picked for the next one.

It is now 12th March, and I have had my leave. We have all been together and I can assure you that I had a very pleasant and enjoyable time at home. The journey back to Windsor was very pleasant, for two of our chaps got in the train at Stockport, and the other chaps in the compartment were quite sociable, so that we had quite an enjoyable time. I arrived at my destination, was fixed up in my new billet, Ashstead House, was in bed by 10pm and had a good night's rest and sleep.

Today, I have been transferred and we have had some stiff drilling, but I am getting nicely on the move in my new company, where everything is new and much more up to date. I shall not be able to write to you as often for the training is more severe, takes up more time, consequently, one has less time for leisure. We have also had a route march, skirmishing in the park, and then items of field training, all of which are done with full pack on. We have had bayonet fighting, constructing various forms of barbed wire entanglements, rifle drill and an actual experiment of smashing up a railway line. The line was laid in the middle of a field to which gun-cotton detonators and fuse were attached. The fuse was then lit and we made for cover. The explosion was terrific and the line was completely smashed. The work is generally more interesting than what we have had previously and I am doing alright.

Rumour has it that we are due out in France on the 26th, but nothing is definitely known. We have been given our draft kit and put in our respective sections. The Brigade is composed of four battalions: The Household Battalion, Seaforths, Irish Fusiliers and Warwicks and is under the command of Brigadier General Pritchard.

A retrospective summary of events falls thus: It is scarcely four months since I joined the Army, and here I stand fully-trained, equipped and ready for the fray. In the ordinary course of events, it would have taken a much longer time, but the pressing needs of our comrades in the field demands speedy preparation. Events have followed each other in such rapid succession that they are almost blurred by their velocity, and look like a moving picture or a screen in which the last impression tends to efface those which went before. What the future has in store for me, I know not. We must do the best we can with the things we come in to contact with, use our intelligence to the best advantage and do what we consider right and proper towards our fellow creatures. Rest assured I go with a good heart, to play a straight game and be a 'man'. I will take my stand side by side with my comrades in arms, in that vast and seething mass of warriors fighting for the cause of right and liberty, and forming a massive khaki line like a barrier rock between our adversary and his dreams on the battlefields of France and Flanders.

Horace (right), with his brother Harold (left) and his father Thomas (centre)

AT WAR-FRANCE.
8th. April, 1917 - *Le Havre*

Excitement and bustle pervaded the atmosphere at Windsor when we were definitely informed that our destination was France. At 9.45am on the morning of 26th. March, we entrained at Windsor and at about noon arrived alongside the quay at Southampton. We detrained and had a look round until 4pm, then went aboard the S.S. Viper. Two hours later, the bridge was drawn and we left the shores of dear old England. On nearing the Isle of Wight, we were joined by the convoying destroyer "Ure" under whose escort we crossed the briny to Le Havre.

The journey was rough in mid-Channel, for the ship rolled, tossed and heaved heavily, and so did my poor stomach, but after feeding the fishes for a short time I felt alright. At midnight, we reached our destination and the ship was made fast to the quay. The night was beautifully clear, and starlit. As I stood on the deck and looked across the river, I saw many various coloured lights across the opposite quay and the thought struck me that this was indeed one of the wonderful sights which one sees but rarely. We disembarked at 7am next morning which opened out bleak and cold, for a raw, cutting March wind was blowing; but, after sorting ourselves out, we had a good steady march to liven us up to our camp at Harfleur, no.1 Infantry Base, which is situated on a high prominence some miles from the harbour.

We are now under canvas and looking straight ahead from our tent door, one sees in the distance the River Seine, with hills receding far beyond it. To the right, the hills seem to rise still higher, whilst to the left in the valley below snugly lies a small town with high hills as its background. Since our arrival here, there has been scarcely anything but rain, with dark clouds hanging heavily around. Occasionally, the sky has cleared and the sun shone brightly which has made the surroundings look very fine. The roads are awfully dirty with the interminable cavalcade of vehicles ceaselessly going to and fro, but one soon gets accustomed to wading through the slush and mire.

Easter week has passed but there was nothing to make one realize its presence for we were on the hill doing our training in the usual way. On Sunday, I was on guard duty, here at the base, which is a more serious business than in England. The sentry carries a gas-helmet slung over his shoulder, bayonet fixed, and during the night time has his rifle charged with live rounds. One of my tours of duty was 3-5am, but there was nothing particular stirring. The silence of the morning was however broken by the peculiar screech of an engine whistle as the train passed along the railway line in the valley below, and every quarter of an hour I could hear the chimes of the town clock. Since our arrival here we have had a new rifle and bayonet, a steel helmet, padded inside, which makes it feel nice and comfortable, a waterproof sheet, a breech-cover which covers the breech of the rifle, bolt, magazine and to protect the rifle generally, and a pouch containing two gas-helmets, one for poison-gas, the other for tear-gas.

During our training here, we have been through the poison and tear gases, thrown live bombs, judged distances, practised taking cover, fired a short musketry course of fifteen rounds and many other things. We are confined to camp at present but I am hoping to have a look around before long. There are canteens of the YMCA and SA for rest and refreshment. On the hill above us, there is a search light which is used at nights, and it is a fine sight to follow its movements as it searches the valley below, and the adjoining hills. Military matters must be kept out of letters. We have church parades on Sundays and Mondays are our washing days. The War news of the last few days has been very good; let us hope it may continue.

Day by day we go through the different phases of a soldier's life in preparing to proceed to the Front, and as the days pass by, we learn more and more of what to expect when the time comes for action. I understand that we leave here soon but when is not exactly known. Of course, the move will be up the line. However, I intend to do my best wherever I go or whatever the circumstances.

It is now Monday, 16th April, and we are under orders to remove tomorrow, but we shall be a few days before we reach our destination. I have passed the Doctor so am preparing to move up the line tomorrow.

Horace & Harold with cousin Christopher and a friend

April, 1917 - *Arras*

Our three week stay at the Base brought forth many new experiences apart from the fact of my living on foreign soil for the first time; living under canvas and under very bad weather conditions was a great change from life in billets, but having been in good health, these changes had very little real effect on me. I soon learned the lesson that being able to adapt oneself to conditions, no matter how unfavourable they may be, was the one and only way of making life worth living.

Having gone through the prescribed Base training, on Tuesday, 17th April, 1917, our draft made preparations for leaving with their intention at some date in the near future of joining our battalion in the field. That afternoon, we marched to Le Havre station some three or four miles away. Arriving at the station, we were allotted our places in the various horse vans of which the train was composed. We devested ourselves of our equipment and as we were not due to begin our journey for an hour, walked around the station. There was nothing particular to see, but walking around was much better than being huddled up in the vans, for we were destined to have enough of that very soon. The chief attractions were coffee stalls, which were well patronised.

About 10 o'clock that night, the train moved off and we said goodbye to Havre. The vans were well crowded, and one had to make oneself as comfortable as one could. Some of the boys sang, some played cards, but I went to sleep. Around 2am, the train came to a stop. Where we happened to be I could not say but as there was a place close by where hot water could be obtained, there was a scramble for it, with which, along with our tea ration, we made a "dixie" of tea which was very acceptable. Inside half an hour, we were on our way again and I once more went to sleep. Close on midday, the train pulled up in Abbeville station where we stayed for an hour. We looked around for coffee stalls, and finding none had to be content with our army rations. From the station, Abbeville looked very inviting, but it was not our good fortune to go through the place.

Late afternoon, our journey was completed, for on arrival at St Pol, we detrained, after a journey lasting something like 18 hours. It had been a rough ride, for horse vans are not the most luxuriant of compartments. There were times when we were whirled away at express speed and others when we merely crawled along. Some of the stretches of rail were not in the best possible condition, for many times it seemed as though the train would topple over. However, we reached our detraining point with stiff limbs, but nevertheless, in good health and spirits.

An hour after our arrival at St Pol, we started our march to Savy, where our Divisional Rest Camp was situated. It was a long, weary march and when darkness came on, it seemed more wearisome as, on account of the inky blackness, one could scarcely see many yards in front. We trudged on and towards midnight, footsore and weary, we reached our camp at Savy. Without arguing the point, we slipped off our packs and in a very short time were sleeping the sleep of the just. This place is some 20 miles behind the firing line and at night one can see the flashes and hear the booming of our heavy guns, which are pounding the enemy's lines. Behind our camp is an aerodrome, and machines are continually buzzing through the air like birds. We stayed at this place for a week, during which time we were not worked hard.

On Sunday, April 22nd, we prepared to move with the

object of joining the battalion at the village of Ambrines, some 12 kilometres away. In the cool of the evening, we moved off from Savy and after passing through Berlette, Pénin and Mazières, reached Ambrines late that night. It appeared that the battalion had only arrived at this place a few hours previously, having come from the offensive operations at Arras. The draft was now split up and I found myself with the 4th Company. Our billets were old barns with straw on the floor for a bed. There were tremendous holes in the walls of our barn and blankets were used as a means of giving it a more dignified and comfortable appearance. Here was another new experience. Next morning, the battalion paraded in the main street of Ambrines and was inspected by the Colonel. The weather during the past few days had been very nice indeed after the recent muddy and inclement weather.

For the next week or so, we were engaged in the various evolutions of infantry in warfare. One day, we had a route march through the surrounding villages which included Lignereuil, Givenchy-le-Noble,Villers-sur-Simon, and Mazières. Villages in France are very much alike, for as one marches along the roads dotted here and there may be seen church spires, all of the same style which invariably denote the existence of a village. From a distance, these villages look very picturesque, but later one cannot help but notice their dilapidated condition. They are in no way as neat and prim as our own villages, and lack those things which make for comfort and convenience. Sanitation is non-existent, while all water has to be drawn from deep wells. The roads are helped by tall trees planted either side at equal distance.

On Saturday, 28th April, we were once again on the move, our destination being Arras, leaving Ambrines in the morning. When we stopped, our huts were composed of semicircular buildings with wood floors and corrugated iron roofs. The next morning saw the last stage in our march to Arras, for we had only 8 kilometres to march and mid-day saw us entering the town. What a sight met our gaze. Almost without exception, buildings of every description had suffered more or less severely from shell-fire. The place was simply a mass of ruins. Passing through the town we saw the Cathedral which had been practically razed to the ground. Strangely enough, the cross on the highest point of the building was intact, seemingly defiant of the evil intentions of men. Our billet was a nunnery near to the station which had escaped to a certain extent the fate of most of the other buildings. Our stay here was to be short for very soon we were to go into the line.

May, 1917 - *Houvin*

Our stay in Arras was of one day's duration only for the battalion was due in the line the following night. In consequence, very little of the town was seen beyond the immediate neighbourhood of the nunnery which was our temporary home and the necessary preparations, which were many, for our turn in the line, had occupied a good share of the time. The soldier, especially on active service, readily learns to get to sleep no matter what his bed may be composed of, for the thunder and roar of the heavy guns behind the building (heard at close quarters for the first time) and the fact that one's body came into contact with no more yielding material than hard boards did not prevent me from sinking into oblivion for some hours at least. I had the experience of learning later that when the body is thoroughly exhausted and the mind weary, one can fall asleep even when standing.

During the forenoon of Monday, divine service was held and conducted by the Church of England chaplain in the basement of the building. The place was crowded and the service very impressive for one wondered what the future had in store. The next fortnight was full of incidents and experiences which were mostly tragic.

Soon after dinner, the companies began to move out of the town to take up their positions in the line, which at that time ran in front of Roeux village. Our company (number 4) detailed for the reserve moved off last. Our route for a quarter of a mile lay along the left bank of the Scarpe and then across the river and out into the village of St Nicholas. A little further on the right of the road, we passed what was left of the village of St Laurent-

Blaugy, and half a mile ahead was a steep railway embankment, at which place we halted for half an hour. So far, the firing of our heavy guns had been the sum total of our actual experience of war. Shell-riven buildings had been seen but one could only imagine how their destruction had come about.

Resuming our way we came to Athies Lock where the Scarpe was again crossed. The village of Fenchy was soon reached, and from this point could be seen the coloured Verey lights, a sure sign that the line was no considerable distance away. Outside Fenchy a steep railway embankment was scaled and after marching along the line for a mile or so, we then struck off to the right and were very soon in the reserve line. Not an enemy shell had come near us (a rare experience) of which we were thankful. The reserve line gave one the impression of being no line at all, but simply a few holes in the ground behind a slight embankment. It was close on midnight and we were tired with our march, but seeing that there was very little cover for us, we decided to dig better holes; after doing so, our friends in the front line kept watch, while we in the reserve slept. Sleeping in a hole was better than on hard boards (but not much)-all the same, we slept soundly.

Just as dawn was breaking, the enemy began a bombardment of our lines which lasted for a couple of hours. The shells burst in front and behind us, but apart from making very many holes in the ground of varying sizes and shapes, no damage was done. This was May Day, 1st May, but I cannot say I was very happy. The atmosphere here was very warm and unhealthy. Daylight revealed to us the fact that the Scarpe was parallel with our line and at no more than 100 yards away. Some 50 yards to our right was Mount Pleasant Hood and looking across the river one could see the ridge behind which our foremost batteries were concealed. This ridge received a great deal of attention from the enemy and was day by day swept from end to end with shells. The weather at this time was very hot during the day, but at night one could scarcely keep warm.

On Thursday, 3rd May, three companies of our battalion were in the attack made on Roeux village. The attack began at dawn, 4am, and very soon the objective was reached, but for some unknown reason the attackers retired from the position gained and in so doing were badly cut up by the German machine-gun fire. The original line was held and our company rushed up to keep the remnants of the attack. The trenches were by no means in a good state, but we set to work to make them tenable. At night, outposts were made in front of the line, each manned by a dozen or so men. The line was but thinly held, but one of two bombing raids kept the enemy unaware of our actual state. Nevertheless, our line was very heavily bombarded but no infantry attack developed. The trenches were badly knocked about, and one night the whole of us in our outpost were more or less buried with earth caused by the concussion from shells bursting too close to be comfortable.

At the end of six days, we were relieved by the Royal Irish Fusiliers. Leaving the line, we crossed the Scarpe and made our abode behind Fampous village, about a couple of miles away from the reserve line, reaching there about midnight to a cup of hot tea. Then rain began to fall, we found what little shelter was possible and prepared to get to sleep. My shelter consisted of a fairly deep hole with my oil sheet over the top to keep out the rain, but much of it was already there. This was a very soft bed-wet soil and clay-and again I slept. Next morning I was very much plastered with soil and clay, and my next comrade was in a similar plight as I. As we gazed at each other, the ludicrousness of our situation appealed to our sense of humour and we laughed merrily. A wash in the Scarpe removed a week's accumulation of dirt and I then felt somewhat refreshed. Hunting for rations and the mail were the next considerations. Although we were so near the line, the mail was brought up. Parcels from home contain much nicer delicacies than bully-beef and biscuits and a letter is often worth more than a meal.

During the day, all were busy in making as comfortable as possible the shelters they had taken up the previous night. Pieces of corrugated iron, lumps of timber, old coats and sandbags were used to make the place habitable. Our position was very exposed due to the countryside being flat, and we could easily see our own shells bursting on the enemy's front line. Batteries on our right and left were shelled but none came very near us. Three days we spent in this place. The nights were employed in carrying up ammunition to the front line, for in a day or two another attempt to take Roeux village was to be made. Going up one night, we were resting in a railway cutting, when a shell burst among the party, killing three and wounding nine.

The casualties in the action on May 3rd had sadly depleted the battalion, and there would be barely 200 went into the line on the night of May 10th. The other battalions were also depleted, but an attack was planned for May 11th which was intended to be a surprise which it truly proved to be. Only those who have had the experience know the feelings of one, who in a very short time must go "over the top". The attack was timed to begin at 7 o'clock in the evening of May 11th. The evident idea was to give the enemy a surprise, take the position, and under cover of darkness which would come an hour later, dig in and consolidate without giving the enemy an exact knowledge of our new positions.

The barrage opened out exactly to time and very soon we were following it up. The Household Battalion was in the centre, the Irish Fusiliers on our right, the Warwicks on our left, whilst the Seaforths and King's Own Royal Lancasters followed up as supports. The enemy trench running along the front of the village was reached with very few casualties and most of the occupants were taken prisoner, but many of the enemy who had taken refuge in the houses gave us a great deal of trouble. Most of the houses were, however, cleared with bombs, and then we dug in right behind the village. Darkness then descended giving the enemy no chance of discovering our position. The enemy aeroplanes were over early next morning but did not locate us, for all day their shells burst well behind us which was the best thing that could happen. A house well behind us had not been cleared overnight as a machine gun was pretty active during the morning. It was, however, soon destroyed by a party of bombers who incidentally set the place on fire. The day passed fairly quickly and that night we were relieved by the 51st (Highland) Division.

Towards three o'clock next morning, we reached a railway embankment near Blaugy and here bivouacked for the night. Each man was served with hot tea, a couple of boiled eggs, and pineapple. We had been sorely tried during the last fortnight. Half an hour later, fully worn out, all sought relief in slumber. Next morning, the mail was distributed and just before dinner, we made for Arras. A fortnight previously over 800 men had left the convent in town, but not more than 120 of us returned. Some were prisoners of war, many had been killed, and very many had been wounded.

Arriving in Arras, we boarded motor-omnibuses, which many times had travelled London and the suburbs. The whole division was to go right back for a complete rest, and our Brigade were destined for a village called Houvin. It was afternoon when we journeyed to the village. The sky was clear, the sun shone brightly and one could hardly imagine the events of but a few days ago. Pleasant homesteads, green fields and pretty flowers-all these spoke of peace and quietude, rest and contentment but alas, not many miles away was barrenness and desolation!

June, 1917 - *Houvigneuil*

We spent the next few weeks in this village. Our Brigade had suffered severely in the April and May offensives at Arras, therefore it was necessary that we should have a thorough rest and that the battalions should be made up to strength before again entering the line. Hence, our coming to Houvin as we inevitably named the place, the full title being rather too big a mouthful. It was in the late afternoon of Sunday, 13th May, that the motor-omnibuses landed us at this pretty village.

Our billets were barns, which had been rigged up for our accommodation and comfort. My experience of beds during the last few weeks had been varied and here was another variety, quite the best I was to have on active service. The beds were arranged in three rows all round the walls of the barn, something similar to the style of the beds on hospital trains. A stout oblong framework with wire netting fastened over it was pretty comfortable. We soon settled down in our new "home" where new laid eggs and fresh milk could always be obtained at the farm.

At the various villages where troops are billeted, Brigade bath houses have been instituted in some fair-sized house or barn. The bath consists of overhead sprays through which pass both hot and cold water. By this means, one can get a decent bath, scrubbing down with the hot and rinsing with the cold water. During the first few days of our stay, we were inspected by the Brigadier, General, Divisional General, and Army Corps Commander, and there was also held a Memorial Service to fallen officers, NCOs and men.

Each morning, it was the custom to take the battalion on the march through the surrounding countryside. The weather at this time was beautifully fine and we marched through scenes of loveliness and beauty. Alas, not many miles away, disorder and destruction were the prevailing features. It was, however, a pleasure to know that there were such places where one could for a time forget the horrible business of war. A halt was called at the village of Etrée-Wamin, where there was a very clear stream. The afternoons were taken up by instruction on the machine-gun, bombing and musketry. It was during our stay at Houvin that I became aware of the presence of pests which take cover in every imaginable crevice and attack one at the most inconvenient times.

On Saturday, May 26th, the Brigade sports were held on the temporary parade ground of the Royal Warwickshire Regiment. The day was fine and well suited to the occasion. The competitors were officers, NCOs and men from our own battalion, the Seaforths, the Royal Irish Fusiliers and the Royal Warwicks. The events included sprint races, pillow fighting, long distance running, tug of war, obstacle-races and officers' jumping turnouts. All the events were closely contested thus providing a very good afternoon's sport. Tea was also provided. The Divisional Band also played selections of music, thus adding much to the day's pleasure. For several nights, some of us slept outside, under the trees in the orchard behind our barn, in peace and comfort, but one night peace was disturbed by a storm at 2am in the morning which continued until noon.

On June 1st, the Divisional Horse Show was held at a village some four miles away. A good number of our battalion went and there were some fine turnouts on view. The officers provided some interesting jumping and we had a good tea on the field. The following day, some boxing contests were arranged which along with the other activities helped relieve the monotony of our ordinary routine. Towards the end of our stay, an inter-platoon competition was decided. Each platoon was to run a mile, march a mile, go over the bayonet course and fire fifteen rounds rapidly at a target. Points were awarded for uniformity in running or marching, smartness in tackling the dummies on the bayonet course, and number of hits on the target and also time in which the journey was accomplished. Our platoon, number 16, made 86 points out of a possible 100 and gained first prize which worked out at five francs per man.

June 12th was the day for our leaving Houvin for a destination which proved to be Arras. Just before noon, we marched and then boarded motor-omnibuses. The month spent at Houvin is full of the happiest recollections. All the sports and competitions had tended to infuse new life into one's blood. Consequently, although the coming weeks would probably be full of danger and apprehension, the change of scene and life would help me to face them with a better heart.

Harold & Nellie Smethurst - Thomas Smethurst - Horace & Mary (Polly) Smethurst

June, 1917 - *Balmoral Camp*

On arrival in Arras, the battalion assembled in an open space and there and then proceeded to dine. About seven o'clock in the evening we moved into our billet, the convent which was being vacated by a battalion of the Rifle Brigade. This was to be our abode for a few days, our battalion being in reserve. The day's routine was fairly easy, for parties of men were required each night for the front line, either to dig trenches or to carry materials for the Engineers.

After two years of ravaging war, Arras was nothing more than a heap of ruins. The most prominent buildings had suffered most: the Cathedral, Hotel-de-Ville and the Station. Even at this time, the town was not immune from being shelled and this usually happened on a Sunday morning. Only a very few French people at this time lived in the town, but there were many troops billeted within its walls.

On Saturday, June 16th, the battalion moved out of Arras and bivouaced on some open ground near St Laurent Blangy. Here, the men set to work and formed what was to be called Balmoral Camp. This was 1$^1/_2$ miles nearer the line than Arras, and was to be one of the places of rest for battalions when relieved in the line. A party of us went that night to take down and collect enemy wire entanglements. A few shells dropped but we accomplished the task without casualties. Next morning, we could see enemy shells bursting in Arras, perhaps a dozen and then all was quiet. For several nights we engaged in digging or carrying materials to the line.

June 22nd found us in the line. We were heavily shelled

on going into the line, the enemy (almost invariably) anticipating the relief. Towards midnight things simmered down considerably and the night passed fairly quietly. The following night, some of our men went bombing and evidently disturbed Fritz for he put down a tremendous bombardment which lasted two hours. Shells of all descriptions burst in all directions until the ground fairly rocked. It seemed as though nothing could live under it and I believe that Mother Earth suffered most. I had the experience of having part of the trench blown in on me by the bursting of a shell dangerously near the parapet. After the storm came the calm, and the dawn found us none the worse for the night's experience.

Behind our lines was an old chemical works, which when in the hands of Fritz, had been used as a shelter for his troops. There was a basement to the works and this provided good cover from shell-fire. At this time, the enemy artillery paid particular attention to this place, evidently thinking (and perhaps correctly) that it was being used to our advantage. After four days in this part of the line, we were relieved by the 12th Manchesters, and our going out was very much like our going in, for we were heavily shelled. Soon after midnight, we arrived at what was generally called the Blue Line, where we were to stay. This was a steep railway embankment running parallel to the line and some three miles away from it. Fine, sand-bagged dug-outs had been made in the embankment, and those were to be our billets when not in the line, for a few months to come. Although nearer the line than Balmoral Camp, it was however, fairly free from shell fire. It so happened that in all our stay at this place, we had only one casualty caused by shell fire.

The camp stretched from the Arras-Fampoux main road to the River Scarpe, a distance of about 400 yards. The bridge which crosses the Scarpe at this point had been blown down in the April offensive and the debris blocked up the river. It was during this time that the place was shelled most but suffered very little damage. For some weeks, the Engineers were involved in clearing the river which saw the advent of small motor boats which were used to carry rations and other things to the reserve line; sometimes the wounded were brought down by means of these boats. From the top of the embankment, the line could easily be seen. We spent eight days here before returning to the line again, and during these periods of "rest" instruction, route marches, and other items formed the daily routine.

On 4th July, we again took our position in the line which had been consolidated after the success of May. Our reconstructed line (battalion front) was really a series of outposts which were gradually connected with one another. Our extreme left rested on the Arras-Douai railway, which at this point seems at a right-angle to our line, whilst the right rested on the River Scarpe. The outpost on the extreme right was the only one not connected up, and was rather isolated. For some reason, this post was never shelled, although sometimes raided. Half of our platoon spent three days in this part, during this particular spell in the line. On account of its isolation, it was always necessary that everyone should be on the look-out at night-time.

About midnight on the second night, we saw a party of Huns bearing down on our post with the evident intent of giving us a surprise and clearing us out. The night was rather dark, but we could see them stealthily creeping up to our wire. As they were attempting to cut our wire and just as we were about to open fire on them, an extraordinary thing happened. Like a bolt from the blue the artillery put over a perfect hail of shrapnel. For some fifteen minutes showers of shrapnel swept the ground between ours and the enemy's lines. Almost as suddenly as it had commenced, the bombardment ceased and all went quiet again. The moon came from behind the clouds and we looked for the enemy, but there was none to be seen. And no wonder! We had not fired a shot and the timely crash of artillery had undoubtedly saved us from having a warm time.

The rest of our tour in the line passed off pretty quietly, with nothing beyond the general routine attached to the work of holding the line, strengthening the trenches, putting up wire, and doing other things which occupied our time. At the end of twelve days, the Seaforths relieved us and we returned to the Blue Line.

July, 1917 - *Blue Line Camp*

It was evident that the camp in the Blue Line had now become a regular abode when out of the line, and although comparatively near the line was fairly safe and did not suffer much from shell fire. We were well dug in the embankment on the opposite side to the line and consequently did not offer much of a target to the enemy guns. When, however, targets did appear shells very soon came over. Such was the case when the Engineers were clearing the debris from the Scarpe, and also on the appearance of a captive balloon. Observation balloons were generally put up round the town of Arras, but one morning, no doubt for the purpose of getting better observation, one was brought up to the Blue Line during the day-time, and lay under cover of the embankment. In the evening, the balloon was put up and had scarcely been up five minutes when a hail of shells were fired at it, some bursting very close. It was deemed advisable to take it down and move it back to its former and safe position.

The better part of a fortnight we spent in the camp. "Out for a rest" signifies rest in the sense of being free from the perils and the attendant contingencies of a term in the trenches only. The mornings are generally occupied in rifle-drilling, instruction in bombing, machine-gun and bayonet fighting. Occasionally, a route march takes the place of the drill. The afternoons are not as fully occupied as the mornings and consequently the day's work is not very hard. There is always, however, the possibility of being one of the party of men going to the line at night to do trench digging or some other jobs.

One day we had a march through one or two of the

surrounding villages. All the fields were full of beautifully tinted flowers and even the trenches which Fritz had occupied only three months previously shared in the glory of nature. It seemed almost impossible that in so short a time what had been a scene of bloodshed and horror could be transformed into such a veritable paradise. Nature healing her wounds could be discerned on every side.

On Saturday night, July 28th, our battalion again took its place in the line behind Roeux. The route to the line was generally along the right bank of the Scarpe. Six days in the line were passed fairly quickly, at the end of which time we were relieved and went into a railway embankment which was termed the brown line and which was just across the river. The second night of our stay, a party of us were engaged in carrying duck-boards and baulks of timber to a dump in the front-line. On going up, our "heavies" put over a bombardment and we were obliged to take cover until Jerry's reply had died down. We then delivered "the goods" and returned to our dug-outs at about one o'clock in the morning. The moon was fully risen and shining brightly. The scene would have been one of utter peace and contentment had not the "heavies" in the woodlands below been flashing and belching forth their missiles of death as they pounded the enemy lines.

August, 1917 - *The Blue Line*

Another short spell out of the trenches is very welcome. Although for the past two months we have been "holding the line", the job is much more exacting than the uninitiated would imagine. On the "quiet" days the trenches are invariably shelled, and at night time one has always to be on the look-out for surprises. Fritz very often raided the isolated outposts, but so far as we were concerned never managed to effect a surprise. Our isolated outpost received a great deal of attention from the enemy in the way of raids. In addition, patrols were sent out to gather information as to the enemy's numbers, and positions. We were also working and moving parties. Under cover of darkness, a tremendous amount of work is accomplished. Barbed-wire entanglements are put in front of the trenches and around the outposts, and the trenches themselves are also strengthened by sandbagging. Rations, ammunition, timber for dug-outs, and "duck-boards" for the bottom of the trenches have all to be carried up to the respective positions in the line by parties of men, very often under shell fire. "Holding the line" is no mere happening and consequently, rest for both mind and body is required in order that the best possible result may be achieved. Drill, sports, amusements and marches through the beautiful country all serve to build up and strengthen the mind and body for further exertions.

The end of the first week in August found us once again at the Blue Line, and for the better part of a fortnight the cares and exactions of war were partially put aside. In our Brigade, the Household Battalion and Seaforth Highlanders were obviously very sociable with each other and often co-operated together in the holding of sports. During this period of rest, the two battalions held swimming sports in the lake in the grounds of the château near our camp. Racing on rafts with the crews using their feet as propellers was a very amusing and keenly contested event. High diving, tug of war, and the "candle race" all contributed their quota to the success of the afternoon. Swimming with the legs and keeping a candle alight constituted the latter event. A keenly contested water-polo match between the officers of the battalions concluded the programme. One incident only occurred-one morning, our company was drilling in a field to the left of the camp when suddenly enemy shells began to burst. The presence of one or two enemy aeroplanes overhead evidently accounted for this disturbance. However, no casualties occurred.

One day, I was sitting on the top of the embankment. Looking towards the river, I noticed a motor-boat gliding down the river in the direction of Arras. Suddenly, a flame burst forth and the boat sank like a stone. Several officers and men who happened to be nearby immediately dived into the river and succeeded in rescuing some of the occupants but several were beyond human aid. The rescued were attended to by our M.O. What was most pathetic was the fact that some of the men were sick going down the line and perhaps to Blighty. How strange is the irony of fate.

The 18th August was the day of our return to the line. The outpost on the banks of the Scarpe was in no good favour with anyone and a strong party of machine gunners and bombers was always sent to man it. The post was divided into two sections, one looking straight ahead to the enemy lines and the other to the right and across the river. The grass in front of this post was high, and along the banks of the river, tall and thickly foliaged trees grew, whilst the river was no more than three yards in width. It can thus be understood how possible it was to effect a surprise and how necessary it was to keep a sharp-lookout. There was a strong barbed-wire entanglement in front of the position thus eliminating to a certain extent, the possibility of a complete frontal surprise.

This post was the one in which sixteen of us were to pass the next four days. Two days was the general rule, although we had volunteered to do the other two days in order to get an extra few days rest. It happened that we had a lively time of it, and were not sorry to get away. Never was the dawn of day more welcome than on this job. In the ordinary trench two men at a time can very well act as sentries to a section, but in outposts the whole section must be thus engaged continuously.

It is no easy matter peering into darkness for hours at a stretch and when all is quiet, one's imagination is apt to run riot. What turns out to be trees in the daylight appear at night to be so many men and what is more, they seem to take life the more one looks. The rustle of the leaves of the trees, or an apparent sound of disturbed water puts one in a state of expectancy. For a whole hour, the artillery may be silent and silence seems to add to time. The crash of shells relieves the mind a little even though our own lives are being shelled. Of course, it is much more so when the missiles are going the other way.

The appearance of the moon from behind the clouds also relieves the monotony in the outpost, although it is a source of danger to those seeking to solve the mysteries of "No Man's Land". The trenches were a quarter of a mile apart at this point and as they were dug in limestone, could be seen by the rays of the moon. At night, on several occasions, parties of Germans were seen carrying picks and spades across the river, evidently going to dig or construct something. When the night was quiet, these men could be distinctly heard shouting to each other and on one particular occasion a chap could be heard sneezing at intervals for an hour or more. A man like that is a danger to a party working between the lines for he is apt to give the show away. I believe the chap was unwell, but he was in danger of getting a pill that would cure him permanently of his troubles.

One night, a small patrol of men went out into "No Man's Land" in front of our post. They had been gone no more than ten minutes when they ran into a large enemy patrol. A few bombs were discharged but our party being outnumbered retired on our post. A minute or two afterwards the enemy patrol was seen bearing down on us, and at no great distance from our wire. We immediately opened fire with machine-guns and rifles and gave them a hot reception. They turned tail and the artillery, having been warned, completed the work with a shower of shrapnel. Being relieved at the end of four days, our small party came out of the line to enjoy the extra four days rest before the whole battalion was relieved. We then went back to Dingwall Camp near to Balmoral Camp constructed in June.

August, 1917 - *Arras*

For four days, our small party at Dingwall Camp enjoyed much more freedom than in general when, with the whole battalion out of the line, football and other games during the day and visits to Arras in the evening afforded us a jolly time, and everyone felt distinctly happy with himself. All good things come to an end sooner or later and so on Sunday evening, August 26th, we moved to the Blue Line, there to join the battalion which had just come from the trenches. For another week or so, the general routine was gone through and during this time rumours were current to the effect that our next turn in the line would be the last on the Arras sector and a visit to a new sector would, of course, be the result. Rumours were ever prevalent among us, most of which never materialized but this one proved to have a good foundation. There was a short rest before our transfer to the other field of operations. Our sector had been fairly quiet for some two months, and a change was considered welcome-not that anyone greatly desired to be "amongst it" but that the change would relieve the monotony.

However, we contented ourselves with our immediate duties, and at least looked forward to withdrawal right away from the line. One or two events during our last "rest" period at the Blue Line are worth relating. One day we marched into Arras, and spent a good part of the day at an excellent rifle-range situated in a kind of fortress in the town. Shooting competitions took place and my platoon succeeded in carrying off one of the prizes which consisted of tins of excellent salmon, and which provided us with a first-rate feast. Saturday, September 1st was the anniversary of the formation of the battalion, so an effort was made to recognise the fact. In the morning, there was an inspection parade at which the Colonel reviewed the work of the battalion during the twelve months of "its existence".

Sports in the afternoon, a fairly decent tea, and a sing-song in the evening sums up the celebration.

The next day-Sunday-saw us on manoeuvres in the countryside around Arras. We were away the whole day and had our field-kitchens with us. The next evening we went to the line and for the next three days had the opportunity of having a last good look at these particular trenches.

Since our previous visit to the line, the Engineers in making dug-outs had broken through into galleries of limestone which had probably been in existence for years. These proved to be very useful as a place of safety, and were very much resorted to. During the day-time, a few men were on sentry duty, the rest being withdrawn from the trenches or outposts and put into these places. The chance of casualties in the trenches was thus reduced to a minimum and although it was rather cold among the limestone, one had the feeling of being safe. At night-time, however, the outposts were fully manned.

The three days passed over fairly quietly, although Fritz was rather too liberal with his gas-shells which were not, however, of a very deadly nature, for which we were very thankful. The gas shelling generally came off in the early morning but I believe we escaped with only one casualty from this. At midnight we were relieved by a battalion of the Cameron Highlanders belonging to the 15th Division which had just come down from Ypres.

Once out of the line and across the river, the battalion assembled to board the train and we started our journey down the line. All were extremely happy for we were going right out of it for Divisional Rest. We sang with happiness:

> *"Boys coming from the firing-line,*
> *Boys coming from the firing-line.*
> *You can hear them shuffling along*
> *You can hear that Sergeant Major shouting*
> *'Come along boys. Get into some sort of line'.*
> *Fell off the rank and file*
> *In the evening by the moonlight*
> *Coming from the firing line".*

We eventually reached a village named Bailleulval. For a fortnight, we enjoyed the quiet of this pretty village. We were to set off to Flanders.

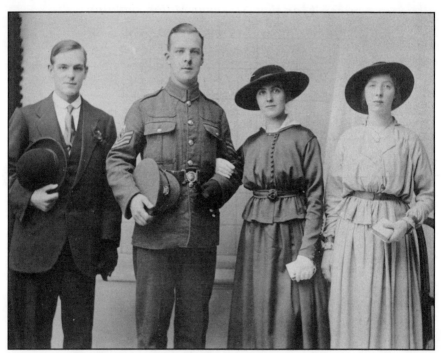

Brother Harold's wedding with Horace as best man and a bridesmaid.

September, 1917 - *Ypres-Boulogne*

Our stay at Bailleulval was a very happy one but all too short. On Wednesday morning, September 19th, we marched out of the village and arrived at Saulty Labrett where we were to entrain for our new sphere of action. We bivouaced in a field near the station, which consisted of a small brick building and proceeded to dine. Near to the station, a number of French people were selling pears which, although 25 centimes each, were eagerly bought by the troops. The fruit was delicious and certainly the finest it has ever been my lot to taste. The mail was also given out and not a little disappointment to the unfortunate ones. The general opinion was that we were bound for the north but the exact place was not known.

In the early afternoon, the battalion entrained and very soon we were in the midst of yet another "joy ride". In due course, St Pol was reached. It appears to be a big railway centre and reminded me very much of Crewe. As night fell, there was very little chance of having an undisturbed nap. We could hear the roar of and see the flashes from our big guns as they bombarded the enemy lines. We came to Hazelrouch where I slept and was only aroused by the shouts and bustle consequent on arrival at our destination-which turned out to be Proven in Belgium. Our journey had lasted about twelve hours.

Very soon we were on the move and after about twenty minutes of marching arrived at a camp which was named Patiala and which was about a mile outside Proven. Kits were quickly dumped and no one seemed anxious to argue. At day-light, the flatness of the country was noticeable. Thus, I came to Belgium for the first time, but I was destined to spend less than a month within its borders.

Proven is not a big place but there was a tremendous amount of railway traffic there and it appeared to be the terminus for vast numbers of troops going to and from the Ypres sector; divisions arriving and leaving daily. For about ten days, we stayed at Proven and the routine was similar to what we generally experienced when "on rest". Ypres is about twelve miles and Poperinghe four miles from Proven. One day when on a route march we passed through the latter town.

Having learned definitely that someone I knew was with the 1st K.O.R.L. Regiment, a unit of our Division (the 4th), I set out from our camp and located him in Sarawak Camp which was situated some three miles from the town. It was a happy meeting and we managed to see each other on two or three other occasions. One afternoon, we held sports near the camp, the majority of the events being on horseback. These events were excellent and the music of the Divisional Band added much to the excitement.

On 25th September, three platoons of our company, including mine, were sent to the 9th Field Coy, Royal Engineers, who were under canvas at Patagonia Camp. This camp was our abode for three days during which time we were inspected by the Divisional General, Major General T.G.Matheson.

On Saturday, 29th September, we entrained at Proven and travelled in the direction of Ypres, detraining at Elverdingle, and from there marching to dug-outs. There were some very fine dug-outs in the banks of the canal, which were necessary as Fritz had a nasty habit of bombing them pretty frequently from his aeroplanes. This was a much livelier place than Arras, for bombing behind the lines was unknown there. However, as on previous occasions, we were forced to make the best of the conditions. The dug-outs were very well filled, for there was no room for equipment which had to be left outside.

A big offensive was looming in the air and our work with the Engineers was concerned with the laying of "duck-board" tracks which were necessary on account of the ground. The country is very flat and shell-holes for miles were practically lip for lip; consequently, tracks had to be made for the passage of the troops, for the main roads are needed for the transport and moreover, these same roads generally received a lot of attention from the enemy artillery. The "duck-board" tracks did not escape the shelling, and were constantly in need of repair. This work is generally done at night-time, so the night after our arrival saw us going up the line in this new sector. The chaps carried up the boards from the "dump" while the Engineers constructed the tracks which were run almost up to the point where our troops were holding the line, or rather a string of shell-holes, for there were no trenches in this part. The first night on this job didn't impress me with the healthiness of the place, but we accomplished our job with no casualties. It was a very long walk to the line from the canal and one felt very tired on arrival back.

The advent of October brought with it a great change of weather, for rain poured in torrents for days. The artillery activity was tremendous, and also that of the aeroplanes. From the canal embankment, I have seen hundreds of aeroplanes up at the same time, enemy and our own and many of the combats were witnessed.

On October 4th, our attack was launched in this sector and from then our work became increasingly difficult, as the enemy knowing the necessity of our making new tracks over the captured ground and also keeping the old tracks in repair, in consequence shelled these tracks heavily and we incurred many casualties.

On the afternoon of 8th October, we rejoined the battalion and moved to a place called Gaiety Farm for we were in reserve for the attack on the 9th. Our bivouac was a field in which were erected a number of canvas tents about three feet high which afforded a covering and did not give any indication of our presence, for the place was comparatively near the line, and aeroplanes, both British and enemy were continually hovering overhead. There had been heavy rain every day since the advent of October and also the nights were cold. The scanty shelter did not do much towards keeping one warm.

The next morning, the 9th, we were aroused and ready for any emergency when the attack began. Our troops were successful and very soon, batches of prisoners came down the line. Towards noon, we moved up towards the front line and "dug in" behind an old windmill, which was no great distance in front of our field batteries. Here, we stayed till dusk, and as we were not required, moved back to Gaiety Farm. The next night, we moved up and took our place in the front line. Going in was a very warm operation, as we were very heavily shelled. The line consisted of a series of shell-holes.

On 12th October, we launched our attack at 5.25am. We had been on the move about twenty minutes and were driving the enemy before us, when I was struck on the head by a piece of shrapnel which penetrated my still-helmet and laid me out. After crawling to a shell-hole, two Fritz prisoners were made to help me towards the dressing station. I was paralysed in both legs and these chaps dragged or carried me for a hundred yards, when we came across a stretcher onto which I was dumped. It was a long and tedious journey to the dressing station, for the roads were in an execrable state, and the Germans were middle-aged men who dumped me down about every twenty yards. Arriving at the dressing station, I was attended to and then, with many more chaps, sent by light-railway down the line. In the evening, I found myself at the 12th Casualty Clearing Station which is near Proven.

In Hospital

On arrival at the Casualty Clearing Station, I was operated on and did not come to until 6 o'clock the next morning when I felt very sick indeed, the result, I suppose, of the chloroform. Hardly a day had elapsed since I had slept in a wet, slimy shell-hole with lice-infested clothes to my back, and a tremendous coating of mud plastered on the outside. Now I was out of it all, with a nice soft bed, clean sheets, and above all, rid of those abominable clothes. The change was great in that I had never been confined to a bed previously and had to lie perfectly flat and must not even lift up my head. For a couple of days, I got little to eat, but later I did the food full justice. Moreover, chicken beats bully-beef and jelly and custard puts jam and marmalade in the shade. The warm and comfortable ward was preferable to the damp, draughty dug-out in the canal embankment, and the effect of the rain which still continued was confined to the noise it made as it dashed on the corrugated iron roof of our ward.

It would hardly be correct to say that we were entirely away from danger, for in this worst of all sectors, bombing by aeroplane was a speciality and every night the droning of the engines of the many planes could be heard quite distinctly. One wondered, rather fearfully what would be the result should bombs be dropped near us. The snappy, rasping sound of the anti-aircraft guns added to the noise, and one felt not a little uncomfortable. At no great distance from here was one of the aerodromes and at about four o'clock every morning one heard the firing of the planes' machine-guns giving warning of their return to roost after a night's bombing.

On Sunday evening, October 21st, I was put aboard a hospital train bound for one of our bases on the coast, and next morning found myself at Boulogne. By motor ambulance, I was taken to one of the hospitals. The sea is not far away and the fresh breezes can be felt. Hospitals are not the dull places one generally imagines them to be. Pain and suffering are there, but in spite of both, the spirit of cheerfulness is also very much in evidence. In our ward was a very intelligent boy from Jamaica. How he loved to speak of his native clime and its store of sugar-cane! He considered Jamaica impregnable and avowed that the Germans would never get there, even if they so wished.

Even at this place, we were not free from the visits of the enemy aeroplanes. Occasionally, they could be heard hovering overhead but were generally cleared off before doing any damage. Four weeks at this hospital, and I found myself on the morning of November 19th ready for my journey back to dear old England. By motor-ambulance we were conveyed to the docks at Boulogne. What a dirty looking place it is. By eight o'clock in the morning, I was in a cot on board the "Princess Elizabeth", a Belgian boat with the Belgian flag flying. My bed was near a port-hole and I could, with a little effort, see the briny and get the full benefit of the ozone. It was noon as we moved off and as the ship left the quay, I wondered whether I should ever visit that land again, and if so, in what capacity. The sea was beautifully calm and I did not experience sea-sickness as on my outward journey. Three destroyers convoyed us across but the journey was without interruption and towards two o'clock in the afternoon, the white cliffs of Dover came in sight.

I have often read of the beauty of those cliffs, but on that November afternoon, they seemed to be the most beautiful things imaginable. I was filled with emotion and thought how beautiful indeed is my native land. I left its shores with far different feelings, not that I did not value my home, or friends, or the land of my birth but simply that a "I must make the best of the job" kind of feeling prevailed. A somewhat similar feeling came over me as the train whirled us up to London. Looking through the carriage window, I saw the beautiful fields, the neat thatched cottages and the blue skies. I had seen beauty in France and Belgium, but it could not appeal to me like this. Towards evening, Charing Cross Station was reached and from here I was despatched to the military hospital at Mile End. So, I was introduced to London.

Our Christmas in hospital was a delight. Everything possible was done to make the time enjoyable and we had a feast good enough for kings. Very soon, I was sent to Dulwich for convalescence. Our "home" was a fairly decent mansion belonging to the Enos of salts fame. Towards the end of January, I returned to Mile End and on February 1st, I was sent on my ten days' sick furlough.

June, 1918

Ten days furlough to the Tommy seems a very long and welcome holiday, but is all too short for he has barely had time to renew old feelings and to pull himself together when he finds himself wending his way back to the regimental depot.

Towards the end of the second week in February, I found myself again at Windsor. It appears that while I was in hospital, after the October offensive at Ypres, the battalion returned to Arras and put in a few turns in the line south of that town before it was split up, the men going to the various Guards Regiments. The men, who were on average big, fine fellows, were undoubtedly quite welcome as reinforcements to the Guards! The regiment was an expensive one to maintain as the men were receiving Household Cavalry pay. However, the end came and as their comrades in France went to swell the ranks of the Guards in the Field, so the reserves at Windsor were being led off to the Guards' Depot at Caterham. Thus, on my arrival at Windsor, there were very few men knocking about, and these were like myself just out of hospital. Moreover, there was a kind of "clearing up" business going on, and it was evident that the place would very soon be entirely "cleared out". However, I spent five happy weeks at Windsor and it was a pleasure to see the daily arrival of many of the boys whom I had once known across the pond.

Early in March, we packed up and went to Caterham. I had scarcely been in the barracks five minutes before I became a Grenadier Guardsman. Immediately on entry, we were drawn up in a line and very soon were marching off to the various quarters of the regiments to which we had been allotted. Here was a fine barracks. If soldiers are ever made, it is surely at the Guards Depot at Caterham. The training is severe, but when one emerges from it, it is as a man knowing his business fully.

The severe fighting in the early part of the year had very much depleted the ranks of the Guards, as also many other regiments, so towards the end of April, the depot was daily filled with recruits. Very soon, the buildings became inadequate to house the newcomers and as the Summer was at hand, camps sprang up in every direction. Very soon the countryside was filled with rows upon rows of white bell-tents and marquees. This outdoor life was preferable to the stuffy buildings now that the fine weather had come. The business of drilling was not my lot for on account of my wound, I had been recommended for discharge and expected any day to go to the discharge centre at Putney.

On Sunday, June 2nd, I said goodbye to Caterham and proceeded to Putney to attend the Medical Board the next day. I received my discharge and made preparations for returning to my native village to take up once more the threads of civil life. Thus ended my brief but active career as a soldier of the greatest army England ever mobilised to take its part in the greatest war the world has ever known.